Corporateocracy

By Curtis R. Crim BA

ISBN: 978-0-615-34804-9

Printed in the United States of America

First Printing

This book is lovingly dedicated to my
children, the true loves of my life.

TABLE OF CONTENTS

Preface

The issue of how to describe the political system of the United States of America is clearly one of political science. However, I am not a political scientist, so one might wonder what qualifications I have, if any, to address the subject of this book.

Although my degree is in Computer Science, I also studied philosophy and cultural anthropology in college, and throughout my life. I am also a corporation behaviorist, and an astute observer of the American culture, in which I have lived my entire life.

As an American citizen, I have watched my culture become diluted, cheapened, and turned into a pale version of what was once great. I am very concerned by the tactics I have seen large corporations use against the American public and the political system of the USA. I have witnessed corporations committing the most heinous crimes one could possibly imagine against God, Creation and Humanity, and get away with them time and again. I have seen my right to vote turned into a commercial for a democracy that no longer exists. I have seen the poor trampled by the aristocracy which shows no signs of moral conscience. I have seen our Federal Government taken over and destroyed by the Multinational Mega-Corporations (MMC's.) I (barely) survived eight years of Republican treason against the people of the USA from the year 2000 until the year 2008.

Quite frankly, I don't even want to write books, nor do I aspire to be an author. I have just become so outraged by the absurd lie that the American culture has become that I feel that I have no choice but to offer my opinion. I believe that if I manage to open the minds of even a few poor commercially-brainwashed individuals, this book is worthwhile and meaningful.

Keep in mind that as an American citizen, you are trained to absorb programming as you watch the television, and are conditioned to believe what you are told, be complacent, and not question reality nor think for yourself. In other words, America is a great place to live if you are a conformist or a conservative, but a living nightmare for people who are independent, use their brains for thinking, or are individual or creative in any way. Liberal thinking is not only discouraged in this sad conform-ocracy, but liberals are generally considered terrorists by the retarded.

My purpose for writing this book is to get Americans to wake up and observe the culture around them, rather than just believe what is being forced into their brains through contact with American culture (i.e. television), which is poison and contaminating. I want people to try to base their understanding of the world on what they see with their eyes, not on what they hear from other people and on TV.

Although I cannot claim to be a political scientist, I am qualified to address the political crisis in America because I am a citizen of the USA who has lived in this country for over forty years, because I am opinionated, and because I type very quickly.

By making scientific observations and recording cultural data over the last forty years, I have made myself a qualified expert on American culture, and I have identified the Multinational Mega-Corporations as the greatest threat to our society, our culture, our system of government, our environment, our lives and the Earth itself. This book addresses the issue of the wholesale destruction of our culture and government by these corporations.

Wikipedia has the following definition: "**Corporatocracy** or **corpocracy** is a form of government where corporations, conglomerates or government entities with private components, control the direction

and governance of a country. This is
sometimes considered to be a form of
fascism." It goes to add that governments
universally fail to aknowldege the term at all.
I chose the term "Corporateocracy" for this
book because I wanted to keep the word
"Corporate" intact. This is a short book
which I hope will appeal to all
demographics of American society,
including those who do not normally read a
lot of books.

Introduction

 The primary question that this book
addresses is: "Is the United States of
America a Democracy?" Once upon a time,
this was true, but the presence of the
Multinational Mega-Corporations (MMC's)
has changed that. The intention of my
argument is to illustrate that the USA is no
longer a Democracy, and that the more
appropriate term to describe our political
system is "Corporateocracy."

Secondly, it is important to understand what
the Multinational Mega-Corporations are,
and clearly see their part in the extinction of
the species Homo sapiens *sapiens*.

I don't plan to dwell on the negative, but
want to propose various solutions to the
corporation problem; a problem that will
result in planetary extinction of almost all
species, plant and animal alike. The threat
that the corporations pose can be addressed
on various levels, including legal, military,
psychological and spiritual.

The goal of this book is to raise awareness
of what the USA has actually become, as
opposed to the vision of America as spun on
the televised network of lies and
brainwashing. If the common citizen

remains complacent, brainwashed, drugged and addicted to "American Culture" as packaged and delivered by the MMC's, then the entire human race is already lost. The re-legislation, reformation and evolution of the Multinational Mega-Corporations are absolutely necessary for life on Earth to become sustainable by the human species.

Chapter 1:
Democracy Killed by Capitalism

To start, we need to get an overview of the current American culture, from the most powerful to the poorest people in our society. For this purpose, it is important to start off by looking at cultural structures within a historical framework.

By observing human societies over the last ten thousand years, one overwhelmingly obvious pattern that arises is the control of society by a few aristocrats who oppress and torment the poor masses. Regardless of the type of culture or political system, one finds that it appears to be inevitable in human society that a few people with a huge amount of wealth and power always end up abusing the majority of the people, destroying their rights and lives for the soul purpose of attaining additional wealth. This is a straight-forward Marxist view of any human society.

However, the whole point of the Democratic system of politics is to "level the playing field", so to speak, and allow poor people to have the same voice in their government as the wealthy. Obviously, with the Electoral College, the USA is not a simple "majority-rules" style democracy. It is a hybrid democracy at best, in which a corrupt electoral college deprives citizens of the proper weight of their vote. Further, the Republicans abused the electoral system and subverted an executive election in the year 2000. As long as the Electoral College exists, perverse aristocrats will always be able to illegally take over the office of the President of the United States.

My objection to the Electoral College aside, the USA is generally described as a democratic society, and ideally every person's vote has equal weight. It is a generally held belief that a poor rural Iowan's vote counts the same as the vote of the CEO of Exxon/Mobile. Historically, the USA has claimed to be a Democracy since its founding in the late 18th century.

However, just because the USA is theoretically and historically a democracy doesn't mean that it is in 2010. As has always happened in human societies, the aristocracy has managed to hijack our democracy and hold it hostage.

The take-over of our government and the destruction of our once-democratic system of politics started after the end of WWII when the USA emerged as a world super-power.

As a democracy, the USA was able to survive comfortably with a common sense of nationalism. However, as an empire, it became apparent to the corporate lords that their greed-based system could not be maintained without a slave class. The problem at that point being that the Emancipation Proclamation prohibits the (outright) owning of humans as slaves.

The wealthy of America have invented many ways to "legally" enslave innocent people. One example is the common practice of imprisoning innocent black men and making them work without pay. This is done very frequently, and is "legal", however clearly against the anti-slavery laws at the same time. One fact that has emerged is that the aristocracy has no obligation whatsoever to obey the law.

In addition to obvious forms of slavery in the USA, I contend and submit to you that a majority of Americans are unknowingly and unwittingly enslaved, and are totally oblivious to their status as slaves.

A true democracy where every person (including the enslaved) gets to vote is clearly unacceptable to the MMC's. One might then wonder if democracy and capitalism can ultimately coexist in the same society.

It appears that this is not the case. As a capitalistic society, the culture of the USA puts an extreme emphasis upon money, wealth, and the attaining of physical possessions such as vehicles and real estate. One can even say that the USA is a greed-based culture. Since the acquisition of wealth is our culture's highest value, people with large amounts of wealth end up with a disproportionate amount of power and influence over our culture and government.

Going back to the Old Testament of the Christians' Holy Bible, one sees that GREED is listed as one of the "Deadly Sins". I personally am spiritual but not religious, and don't want to place too much weight on this ancient text, nor do I want to appear to be "preaching", but I do think that the author of this part of the Bible got it right.

American culture is primarily based upon a value that has been defined as sinful for thousands of years. It is certainly easy to see how non-Americans can view the culture of the USA as being evil.

Capitalism inevitably produces a greed-based and therefore an evil-based culture. A greed-based culture is by its very nature corrupt. Because money is the most valued thing in our society, one can hardly expect politicians to be virtuous and maintain a perfect record of turning down bribes offered them by the wealthy.

Because of this inherent evil of a Capitalistic society, the power of money will always serve to subvert the ideals of Democracy.

Although we in America use the term "Democracy" casually and not very accurately, it is clear that Capitalism, not Democracy, controls our government. Capitalism, therefore, has become our political system, not just our system of economy.

Because greed and money control our politics, Democracy does not exist in America. The aristocracy use their corporations to control every aspect of our culture and our government, and it is my observation that the governments of the USA, both local and Federal, serve the interests of the corporations that exploit the people. The Federal Government has become a flaccid, impotent tool used by the corporations to commit crimes against the citizens of the USA. Our government, like the MMC's, has become the enemy of the American public, and refuses to lift a finger for the good of the common person. It spins the lies and brainwashing that are beneficial to the MMC's, and looks the other way as serious crimes take the lives of innocent American citizens.

The USA, a once-democratic nation, is now in a state of catastrophe, in which a few decadent corporate lords are victimizing the majority of American citizens, committing treason on an hourly basis, and are lying to the masses about the situation. The worst part is that they are getting away with it.

After the funeral of Democracy in America, we find that our Federal Government is now of, for, and by the Multinational Mega-Corporations. The United States of America has devolved from a Democracy into a Corporateocracy.

Chapter 2:
The Legal Problem with Corporations

The legal entity of the corporation was born innocently as a means of organizing groups of people to accomplish a common goal. The corporation allows a number of people working together to been seen as an individual entity in the eyes of the law. The first corporation in America was a company which was hired by the Federal Government to build a large bridge. The corporation was formed so that the people building the bridge could contract for the government for the purpose of this endeavor.

Originally, corporations also had very little power. They could own property, but they had very little influence politically. Over time, corporations have been given increasing amounts of power by the American legislature. This is how the corporate lords took over America.

Corporations that sell shares publicly are very different from purely private corporations. Based on the way they are defined legally, corporations with publicly owned shares are obligated to devote themselves to the profit of their shareholders.

This has lead to profit being their highest motivation.

The problem is that profit has also become their *only* motivation. One might think that devotion to the existence of the human species or to the Earth's biosphere would also be high priorities for any responsible company, but neither of these values has found any place in those of the MMC's. One might also think that common sense would dictate that obeying the law would automatically be a high motivation of any person, corporation or legal entity, but the desire for profit has subverted any motivation for corporations to obey the law.

When a corporation breaks the law, the only thing that our government can do to punish them to is levy a fine. This is meaningless to corporations. They calculate their profit margin to be large enough that they will make money even if they are caught and fined for their illegal behavior. In other words, the only punishment for corporations is no punishment at all, thus they are completely out of control, and are free to abuse humanity and the planet in any way that makes them a profit.

One would not think that it would be necessary, because by definition the law should be obeyed, however, there is no specific legislation that requires corporations to obey the law. There is no legislation that says that corporations have to nurture Humanity or the Earth's biosphere.

As a result, we have ended up with corporations whose only motivation is profit, which is seen as being more important than the law, Humanity and the environment. This makes corporations sociopathic monsters. The following is a list of the priorities and motivations of the MMC's as they now exist:

1) Profit.

That is the whole list. I hope that it is obvious to you that this leads to various ramifications that will bring about the end of life on Earth as we know it.

The MMC's are not only willing but also eager to destroy Humanity for the sake of profit. They have proved countless times that they are willing to destroy the planet on which we live. They prove continually every day that they are willing to break every law of our land for the sake of profit, including committing acts of treason against the USA.

The MMC's, in all their greed, were so motivated by profit that they needed more legislation to give them increasing amounts of power.

The MMC's, in their mad lust for power, bribed senators and representatives alike to pass legislation to allow corporations to own other corporations. That was a huge mistake. It allowed the corporations to spin completely out of control, and to grow in power to the point that they are now more powerful than our government.

Obviously, if a government is to govern its people, it must be the most powerful body in society. Unfortunately, in America we now have many corporations (like Exxon/Mobile) that are FAR more powerful than our government. They are in fact more powerful than any government, and therefore are monsters. They are destructive creatures with no conscience to control their behavior, and their power is without limit.

This ridiculous amount of power was not enough to satiate the corporate lust. The evil traitorous corporation Monsanto bribed senators and representatives to pass legislation that allows them to own patents on DNA. This is also a horrible mistake. Normally, only God can own and control DNA. By attaining the power to manipulate DNA and own a patent on it, the corporations have now made themselves as powerful as Gods. I certainly hope that without help you can see for yourself that any entity in creation becoming as powerful as or more powerful than God is a BAD THING!

The MMC's now have the power to wipe out Humanity completely, and they have no way to practice self-control, nor are they controllable by individual people or governments.

To summarize, the problem with the way corporations are legislated is that they are given infinite power, and no means of controlling their behavior in terms of appropriate moral standards.

Chapter 3:
The Moral Problem with Corporations

Massive Multinational Mega-Corporations' moral problem is rooted in the way they are legislated. Unfortunately, this inappropriate legislation of corporations has led to inescapable immoral behavior.

The MMC's have become monsters that are bent on their own destruction, and the destruction of mankind. How then it is possible for their conscience to condone the extinction of Humanity?

The corporations have no conscience. They have been born and created in such a way that they have no motivation at all other than profit, even to the point that they murder everything created by God. This makes MMC's the hand of Satan. Because corporations care about NOTHING but profit, they are also happy to kill God if possible, for the sake of profit. Corporations have no way to distinguish right from wrong. They are blind as to everything but profit.

By attempting to kill everything in creation, the corporations are attempting to kill God for money and power.

Even though the cause of the immorality of corporations is the way they are legislated, they should take responsibility for their behavior, and have the fortitude of heart to do what is correct irregardless of their legal obligations.

The MMC's, ultimately, have to decide for themselves what is right and what is wrong, because the government has no control over them. Ideally, the MMC's would see the obvious fact that if they kill all humans on this planet, they will have killed themselves as well. However, the corporations lack logic as well as self-control, so their mad lust for profit trumps any form of intelligence that would lead them to not be self-exterminating.

One would think that the corporations would see that they need to make caring for Humanity and the environment their highest priorities, but greed leads inevitably to intense retardation to the extent that the short-term desire for profit supercedes the desire for profit and health in the long run.

The conclusion is that MMC's are not only without any kind of conscience, but they are also lacking in any kind of intelligence. If the corporations are allowed to remain completely out of control, they will definitely destroy all life on the planet Earth. When they accomplish this goal, they will not feel bad about it. They won't feel anything at all. Corporations have no ability to feel as do human beings.

Corporations do experience addiction. Profit is heroine to corporations. This is part of what makes them dangerous. When addicted to a narcotic drug, people will behave in ways that otherwise they would find unacceptable. The addiction itself causes them to behave without restraint, and without any regards to the concepts of right and wrong. The same can be said for corporations and their addiction to profit. They literally cannot control themselves. They are so addicted to power that they are high on it all of the time. They are stoned out of their minds to the point where all they can do is get their next fix, and not worry in any way about whether what they are doing is right or wrong. They have no concept of morality at all.

Concepts like decency, good, helping, kindness and charity are completely foreign to corporations. They have no ability to evaluate their own behavior in terms of morality. They also have no motivation at all to foster morals in their scheme of values. They are very literally (as well as metaphorically) the hand of Satan on Earth.

They are the embodiment of evil, and behavior without restraint. As they stand right now, corporations cannot be allowed to continue to exist, with the consequence being the annihilation of all people on this planet.

We have now been given the choice between the existence of Humanity, OR (this is a mutually exclusive "or") the existence of the MMC's. As an individual, you are now faced with the choice between the lives of these mass-murdering monsters, or your own life. There is room on this planet for Humanity OR MMC's, but not both.

Clearly, it is the Multinational Mega-Corporations that must be wiped out in order for Humanity to survive.

It is our charge as responsible, mature human beings to bring about the utter destruction of the MMC's like Pepsi, Exxon/Mobile, Halliburton and Monsanto. Since the survival of the entire human species is at stake, we have to take on this challenge with all due enthusiasm. We cannot afford to be ineffective. We must act ruthlessly in order to give Humanity a chance, even a remote chance, to survive.

Chapter 4:
Solutions to the Corporation Problem

For the sake of the argument of this chapter, I will stipulate that the existence of corporations is mutually exclusive with the existence of Humanity. I am stipulating that the corporations must be exterminated for the sake of the survival of mankind. The question is how to destroy vampiristic monsters that are more powerful than governments, and are nearly as powerful as Gods? The answer I will provide, but that we must fight them in every way possible, and with every fiber of our beings, using every available resource is imperative. Since they MUST be destroyed, HOW is important, but keep in mind that attaining this goal is absolutely necessary. Some of the various approaches that come to mind are psychological, legal, military, and spiritual.

One of the most powerful weapons in the arsenal of the MMC's used to murder people is the advertising industry of America. The lies, brainwashing and manipulation of the advertising industry have a profound and very powerful effect on the population of the USA. Their attack upon our consciousness is on a psychological level, and we must learn to protect ourselves on that level, as well as use this weapon against our enemies; we cannot afford to fail to use this tactic against them. The corporations are comprised of human beings, and humans are easily manipulated and brainwashed. By affecting the thinking of the employees of the corporations, we can directly attack the corporations on a level that will make self-defense more difficult for them. Of course, corporations brainwash their employees all of the time, and attempt to control the flow of information to, and thoughts of, their employees. One of the major disadvantages of working for corporations is that they attempt to control the behavior, feelings and thoughts of their employees. They lie to their employees constantly (and so does OSHA). Wal-Mart is an excellent example of a corporation that continually lies to its employees, and attempts to control their behavior and thoughts as well. This is clearly very evil behavior on the part of Wal-Mart, but then Wal-Mart is the right hand of Satan. One of the best ways to destroy a corporation is to win over its employees, and convince them to strike or sabotage the corporation from the inside. As human enemies of corporations, we cannot ignore the employees of corporations as our potential allies.

The advertisements seen on television are a massive attack of propaganda upon the consciousness of the American public. The pen is much mightier than the sword, and the word of propaganda is among the most powerful of any in history. Any weapon used by corporations against Humanity must be turned upon these evil monsters. They use propaganda to brainwash Americans constantly. We must embrace this weapon and use it against those monsters that would see all of Humanity destroyed. The simple fact is that all contact with human culture and all words spoken by humans are propaganda and brainwashing. If a person says, "this pop is delicious", they are expressing their opinion, but it is also brainwashing. An intelligent approach to contact with humans is to assume that every word spoken is a lie; every word is an attempt at brainwashing. My personal strategy is to never believe a word I hear, and certainly never believe anything in a television commercial. An effective attack upon the enemies of mankind must incorporate a change in consciousness, a change in the collective psychology of Humanity.

Using the advertising industry, the MMC's have poured billions of dollars into building public confidence in the names of their products. I believe that a direct attack on those brand names could be an effective means to damaging a corporation. Everything that can be done to associate the concept of poison with Coke helps to damage the name of that product in the eyes of the public. If you want to hurt a corporation, then hurt its brand names. If they are going to poison people and lie about it, then that is the very least that they deserve. When you destroy a company's brand name, you destroy the capital which they have invested in building up that brand name.

One obvious approach to solving the corporation problem is on the level of legislation. This is, after all, the root of their evil nature. In order to produce a positive change in the nature of corporations, one option is to modify the way they are created in the eyes of the law. Ideally, their goals would be redefined in terms of their legal obligations. If the law were to require corporations to make the existence of Humanity their highest priority, then the corporation itself would become an entirely different entity. If it were possible (and it is, theoretically) to impose legislation upon the MMC's that requires their obligations to be different, then it would be possible to change them into positive entities in society rather than destructive ones.

It is not acceptable for corporations to be more powerful than governments, so the amendment that allows them to own other corporations must be repealed. I am completely convinced that Humanity is doomed so long as corporations can own other corporations. This legislation is one of the nails in the coffin of Humanity. This situation would never have come to pass if corporations were not the tool of Evil itself. MMC's have bribed Republican congressmen to give them more power than our government. Because entities this powerful are a danger to everything in creation, it becomes apparent that nothing can be allowed to have such massive and uncontrollable power. The corporations must be castrated, metaphorically speaking. Their potency must be removed, and they must be made into manageable members of society. In order to remove a majority of their power, the corporations must have the ability to own other corporations removed legally. This is one of the steps that is absolutely necessary in order for Humanity to survive.

Engineering DNA might very well seem to be a major step in the evolution of human technology, but as a scientist I can tell you that it is a really bad idea. I understand deeply the advantages and possibilities of genetic engineering, but obviously it is also a very dangerous practice. Humans have never had the luxury of claiming to be a perfectly moral species. Genetic engineering is a very powerful technology, and in the hands of a species that is by its nature evil and corrupt, it is only going to lead to the unleashing of destructive forces that we can neither anticipate nor control. Even the motivation of profit is not sufficient to mess with a power as dangerous as this. The ability to own a patent on DNA is something exclusively for God; it is not acceptable for corporations to have power equal to God. This legislation is treason against all of Humanity, God and creation, and it must be repealed. Removing the power of a corporation to hold a patent on DNA is one of the required steps to secure the future of mankind.

Here is an example of how genetic engineering can be perverted to create a terrifying prospect: imagine a hypothetical scenario where Monsanto "lobbies" congress to allow them to own a patent on genetically engineered human DNA, and they start research and development on strains of human DNA that are customized for use as slaves, prostitutes and a food source. It is not acceptable for the MMC's to see human beings as a commodity, and that is one of the moral red flags that these

monsters send up. The MMC's *do* see
Humanity as a commodity.

The most important piece of legislation to
pass is an amendment that prohibits any
EVIL DEVIL who has ever or does work for
Monsanto from serving on any
governmental regulatory commission. After
all, these commissions were created to
protect the American people from Monsanto.
Due to the sloppy genetic engineering of
Monsanto, and their lack of vision as to the
broad range impact of the poisonous
engineered crops on the environment, it is
estimated that in less than ten years the
Earth will no longer be able to produce food.
If you have a neighbor who plants Monsanto
seed, you will have to burn them out.
Monsanto has treated the government of
North Dakota and the country of Mexico as
though they are slaves. Any corporation who
can treat governments like helpless animals
cannot be allowed to survive.

The MMC's have used their influence to
make congress make them more powerful
than governments, and as powerful as Gods.
Legislation must be used to remove these
powers from the corporations, and turn them
into entities that are controllable by society.

It has been clearly demonstrated that fining
corporations for their crimes has no effect

on them whatsoever. However, it is legally possible to revoke their corporate charters. For instance, after the illegal takeover of the USA by Exxon/Mobile in the year 2000, the government should have simply dissolved the corporation and revoked their corporate charter, so that they could not continue to commit treason against the USA. There is no way this would have happened, because Exxon/Mobile had total control over all three branches of the USA Federal Government through the traitorous Republican Party at that time. Republicans will point their fingers at everyone except the enemies of America, like the evil Saudi royal family, and Heinz, for that matter. If our government has any control over the corporations, a solution to their existence is at hand.

However, the government has proven that it is utterly under the control of the MMC's, and there is no way we will ever see a legal solution. This is very unfortunate, as a legislative solution would be both legal and the healthiest solution for our culture. I am concluding that this will never happen because the USA Federal Government is now the helpless impotent puppet of the MMC's, used exclusively for their profit and their insane hunger for power. The people of America no longer have a government. They only have a slave-master who serves their enemies. The MMC's have a government that they allow to appear to control the country; the people of America have no government at all. It was stolen from us by white aristocratic slime.

Sadly, it might very well come to an issue of military power to protect Humanity from monsters like Tyson's and Coke. The kinds of strategies that should be employed against the MMC's are both theoretical, and practical.

Corporations enjoy being seen as individuals in the eyes of the law. This is good. When aspiring to destroy one's enemy, it is wise to turn every advantage of one's enemy into a liability. The corporations want to be seen as individuals, so we will do exactly that. Let us expand the metaphor of a corporation as a human body to examine some of the ways to destroy that body. The word corporation is derived from the word "corpse" which translates from the Latin "Corpus" as "body". Let us imagine how we might attack such a body.

The body of a corporation is like a human body in many ways. Crude oil is its lifeblood. Computers are its brain. The physical assets of a corporation are its limbs. The human employees are like parasites or bacteria infesting the body. The human parasites eventually will become the infection that destroys the body, when they sabotage the body from the inside. Electricity is the air that the corporation breaths. These are all essential elements of the corporation that must be destroyed for that corporation to pay its debt to society for its criminal behavior. The ability of the corporation to telecommunicate must also be destroyed. If you plan to kill a human, depriving them of blood and oxygen will certainly kill them. This will also work on a corporation. Without electricity, they will have no computers. The modern day corporation is completely dependent upon computers. Without computers and the internet, they can't even go about performing basic daily banking transactions. If you take their computers (by taking their electricity), you also deprive them of money, and therefore power. Without their capital, they can't even bribe a congressman, so they are truly rendered powerless.

Nuclear warfare is very effective against corporations, because it can be used to destroy their physical and real assets. I strongly advise the use of nuclear devices against MMC's at every opportunity for two reasons: they have no defense against it, and such devices are comprehensive in the scope of their effectiveness. Any human losses are completely acceptable in view of the fact that the option is the extinction of Humanity. I am calling for the utter destruction of the world-wide oil industry, as well as the chemical, transportation, fast-junk, soda pop (High Fructose Corn Poison), advertising, and "food" industries. The people working for these industries are acceptable losses. When one chooses to work for a corporation, he has made his death an acceptable loss. The employees of corporations have no value in terms of being forms of life. They gave up any morality when they chose to work for a corporation. Of course, they are actually just slaves, but like soldiers, they should make the decision to ignore orders when the orders are morally wrong.

I am personally convinced that in some extreme cases, corporations will not be able to evolve to become "gainfully employed" members of society. Many corporations, Pepsi, as one possible example, will never accept their new position as decent members of society, and will persist in committing mass murder. In these cases, the actual military destruction of the corporation will be necessary. The corporation campuses will need to be surrounded, their communications cut off, and their officers and board members executed. I highly recommend air support, as some executives will attempt to escape using helicopters and small private aircraft. A well-trained soldier is conditioned to shoot a target and not consider the morality of the order he received. Similarly, we must see the corporation as a target, and not consider the humanity.

I confess that corporations are purely evil, and the product of the powers of Satan. I personally am not religious, but growing up in a greedy-evil culture like America, I certainly believe in Satan and evil.

Because corporations are produced from the pure energy of Satan's evil, they can also be fought on the level of good. If you pray, you are helping to destroy the corporations. You don't have to be specific, you only have to focus your attention on good, and it automatically serves to destroy Coke, Pepsi and McDonalds. If you meditate, it will help to counteract the influence of corporations. If you give money to charity, it helps to counteract the cold-heartedness of the MMC's. If you raise your own food, it helps to work against the enemies of mankind. These are all small actions, but anything that you do to encourage good also serves to destroy that which is evil, i.e. the MMC's. Unless you are evil, anything that you do helps to defeat the enemies of the human species. This is what is so beautiful about this approach: all one has to do is to effortlessly follow their natural inclination,

and one can help in the war to save
Humanity from the evil vampiristic
corporations.

Boycotts are also effective. This is a simple
step that any American can take, although it
does require some very strong self-control. I
know that it is hard to avoid McDonalds
when you have a strong urge to indulge your
addiction to the dangerous narcotic drug
High Fructose Corn Poison (HFCP), but if
one is successful, it is very rewarding to
know that one conquered one's weakness. I
know that this is not by any means an easy
solution, but if and when a person can rise to
muster the personal strength, it is important
to NOT give your money to any pop
corporation, Wal-Mart, any fast junk saloon
(like McDonalds) or allow one's self to be
controlled by the American advertising
industry.

The stocks of MMC's should also be
boycotted. If you can destroy the value of a
corporation's stocks, then you can also
destroy that corporation. I know that most
people who have enough money to invest in
the stock market are also under the control
of greed, but if at all possible the stocks of
the traitors of America (like the oil
corporations) should be totally boycotted on
the stock market.

MMC's are very powerful, and a major part of their scheme of brainwashing is to convince you that you are powerless. Our culture has some basis for believing that an individual can make a difference in his government, including participating in revolution, but the brainwashing of the corporations clearly dictates that no one can fight a corporation. This is not reality; this is their manipulation attempting to force you to believe that corporations are invincible. Our culture is heavily programmed to manipulate every citizen into believing that they can fight the government if necessary, but that no one can ever fight a corporation. This is just a lie. It serves their purposes, but has no basis in reality. You are a living person, and therefore have a power of consciousness that cannot be taken from you, not even in death. Resolve to throw your spirit against these monsters, regardless of what it takes. They can murder you, your government and your family, but in the end they can never take your will. Always keep in mind that corporations are the enemy of life and God. Live as an instrument of good, and always live for the destruction of the MMC's.

Chapter 5:
Future Evolution of Corporations

I have now discussed the appropriate way to deal with the serial-killing, mass-murdering, sociopathic, traitorous, psychopathic, monster corporations like Monsanto. However, I believe that there is also some value in considering other, more non-violent means to solving the corporation problem.

In fact, now that we have gotten past the emotionally charged hump of this book, I want to direct attention to solutions based on a more positive perspective.

For one thing, I have painted a picture of purely evil corporate behavior, with greed the primary motivating force. In fact, human culture in America as well as on the Earth in general, has already started to take the first steps in evolving to become part of the solution, the sustainable future of Humanity.

One of the biggest steps in accomplishing the goal of human survival is the turning of the tide of collective human consciousness. The fact that some corporations are already on the "Green Scale" measure demonstrates that there is some hope for them.

I have ranted on with great passion about how evil corporations are, where in fact some of them have already proven that my sweeping prejudice against them is at least partially misguided.

As I try to open my readers' minds to the concept of corporations becoming "green" and helping Humanity to survive rather than helping it to become extinct, some slightly more enlightened corporations have already taken the first steps that indicate that evil corporations like Exxon/Mobile are archaic relics of the Age of Ignorance.

I find it not only encouraging but absolutely optimistic that some few corporations have already started to take the steps that I would otherwise plan to suggest myself. I truly didn't expect to see corporations starting to behave like moral, beings with a conscience. Quite to my surprise, the initiative has already started before I have published a word. I am sincerely shocked, and welcome such self-motivated change on their part.

We are going to examine a whole new vision of what corporations can be in the future. What we clearly see now is a bunch of mass-murdering monsters. The vision of the future is much brighter, at least in terms of the possibility of MMC's evolving to become decent members of society.

Out of anger and frustration, I wrote the last chapter based on the perspective that the MMC's are hopeless servants of pure evil, but let us now consider the possibility that this is not the case.

It is very likely that we will see that some corporations are very evil, some that are in the middle-ground, and some hardly evil at all. From this point forward, I plan to consider a more optimistic perspective in which MMC's can become part of the solution, not just the cause of the inevitable extinction of Humanity.

We are now in the enviable position of being witnesses to a major event in the evolution of human culture. I am not considering that some few corporations are inherently evil, but rather I am now considering that some corporations are not.

The simple fact is that a great majority of people refuse to use any creativity that has been given to them. A great majority of corporations are the same way. They are self-convinced that they MUST be destructive to life and the environment, and they are not able to consider any other possibilities.

I am personally convinced that corporations with the necessary will and motivation can make themselves part of the future of mankind. It is possible that corporations can form a symbiotic relationship with the Earth and with Humanity.

The MMC's have always taken the role of a parasite, preying upon Humanity as though it is a victim to been consumed. They also have a parasitic relationship with the environment. The corporations are vampires, sucking the life out of Mother Earth.

Here is my vision for what a corporation will be in the future: It will not be able to own other corporations, nor own patents on DNA, nor illegally manipulate the Federal government. It will not pollute or destroy the environment. It will not be dishonest or abuse Humanity. The enlightened corporation will be entirely different from the bloodsucking monsters that we see today.

Corporations are also a reflection of human collective consciousness. As Humanity evolves towards enlightenment, the corporations will also experience a shift in consciousness, and they will be forced to change. It is an inevitable process which the corporations are helpless to stop.

All over America the Green Revolution is snowballing, and growing at an increasingly fast pace. More and more companies and corporations are becoming aware of the necessity for change. Some are actually evolving to do less harm, while others are just pretending to do so.

To the evil corporations and the advertising industry, the natural inclination is to pretend to be going green, and present the appearance of being more environmentally healthy, where actually they are just lying about it. This is actually a good sign, because they are acknowledging the change in collective consciousness, and the desire of the majority of people to see them change.

The following are examples of corporations PRETENDING to offer healthier solutions, where actually they are just lying about it.

A few years ago, McDonalds came up with a new line of "healthy" salads. You might remember this, as many Americans will have seen the commercials for them. Upon careful analysis of these so-called healthy salads, I found that they are actually just fast junk filled with narcotic poison. The salad I examined had cranberries and walnuts, both of which were sugar-coated and contained HFCP. The salad dressing is also loaded with HFCP. This "healthy" salad was no more than the same poison that they usually sell dressed up to LOOK like healthy food. These salads in fact are not healthy at all, but are the same fast junk that McDonald's typically sells.

Even pop corporations like Coca-cola have changed their labels to make their products appear healthier, and say as much on the label, where in fact the second ingredient after water is the dangerous narcotic High Fructose Corn Poison. The new Cherry 7-Up is one good example of this. It is the same poison that they have always sold, but now it displays lies on the label that say that it is good for you.

Swanson's Vegetable Broth also contains HFCP. This is particularly evil, because most vegans have no desire to poison themselves and destroy their livers with a dangerous addictive narcotic substance. Ironically, the Swanson's 100% natural chicken broth actually *is* 100% natural, and doesn't contain any HFCP. I find this curious because both products are made and sold by the same company.

The American food industry has an amazing ability to make the "food" they produce appear any way they wish. The appearance of "food" is not as important as the substance, so beware of any packaging or presentation that claims that the product is "healthy". Read the ingredients and decide for yourself whether something is healthy or just dressed up to create that appearance. The automatic reaction for most evil corporations is to see the need to become a green corporation, and then produce a deceptive appearance while in fact they remain as malevolent as ever.

Not all companies are like that. The change in the collective consciousness is now becoming more apparent, as more companies are initiating the process of growing green. One example of this is the use of recycled packing material in lieu of Styrofoam packing. More corporations are learning to produce their own resources, produce less waste in the environment, recycle their own waste products, and be less dependent upon non-renewable energy resources.

I found a very cool sight on the internet: http://www.dotgreen.org/. It announces the new .green domain extension. I take this as yet another sign of the shift in the collective consciousness towards becoming a more enlightened species, one that lives harmoniously with the environment rather that destroying it.

The next step appears to be to look into the details of how various kinds of companies can grow green.

Chapter 6:
Transforming the MMC's

For a corporation to have a future on the planet Earth, they will have to grow green. This creates a different challenge for different types of companies. The greening process is entirely different for retail money order companies than it is for energy corporations. This chapter will discuss various kinds of companies and corporations, and some of the specific approaches they might use to become a symbiotic part of the Earth's ecosystem.

I normally charge companies to consult on their greening process, but in this book I am going to give away my consultation service free. I will give a few suggestions as to how specific companies can acclimate to a world of enlightened humans.

To start off with, I want to discuss one of the companies that I take many shots at for being evil: Pepsi Cola. The people at Pepsi can feel free to take my advice to heart, or completely ignore it. I am going to put myself in the hypothetical position of having been hired by Pepsi to show them what it will take to be part of the future of the Earth.

First of all, they need to change their product line. One easy step (for Coke as well) is to go back to a previous recipe for their soda pop that does not contain HFCP. Heck, Coke used to put cocaine in their product, and it was more natural and less addictive than HFCP! Anyway, both of these soda pop corporations have recipes that don't include dangerous narcotics, so they can go back to producing those as new product lines are developed.

I understand that putting a product in a pretty can and displaying the word "healthy" on the label is very nice for advertising, but what goes inside the can is also going to need to be acceptable in terms of being healthy. "New Organic Pepsi" will have to be a theme for the envisioned new product line. Pepsi can purchase raw organic sugar from Hawaii, and use that to sweeten their soft drink instead of HFCP. They can go to using natural coloring and flavoring agents rather than artificial ones. They can even set up a machine to run their water through a reverse osmosis filter system before adding it to the product. I understand that natural ingredients are more expensive, and that the profit margin on this product would not be what they get on their HFCP filled product of today. However, for the sake of becoming a green company, it will be well worth the sacrifice.

Transportation of soda pop is also a major consideration. Coke currently has the largest fleet of vehicles on the entire planet: their delivery truck fleet. The Pepsi and Coke delivery trucks mostly run on diesel fuel. The diesel engine was originally designed to run on soybean oil, which is far better than using refined crude oil. Changing the delivery process will take much more time than changing a recipe, which can be done in under a year. The greening process will take a decade or two for many corporations, to get them up to a full ten star rating on the Green Scale. New technologies will have to be developed, which will slow down the process.

In order to get Pepsi to a full ten star green rating, we are going to have to redesign the engines of their delivery trucks. I am going to go straight to the ideal: pure electric engines. These will need massive battery cells, because the load that such a truck pulls requires enormous amounts of energy. The batteries must have high capacity and be light weight so that they are not a burden on the load. They will, of course, be rechargeable, and Pepsi will need to engineer large solar farms that will produce the electricity needed to recharge their delivery trucks.

There are many tiny details too, like how offices are run, and what food to offer in the employee lunchroom. The best advice I can give is that Pepsi should make sure that they don't have any pop machines available to the employees, because the impact on the employees' health costs the corporation hundreds of thousands of dollars on an annual basis.

I guess I like taking on a challenge, so I am going to take on the big boy of the fast junk saloons next: McDonalds.

This is going to be an insane overhaul! McDonalds is owned by Coca Cola Corporation, and is almost the stereotypical embodiment of the vision of an evil fast junk corporation in America. It is almost beyond what one could conceive that such an entity can grow green, but I think that they can. They have a lot of money and power, so with the desire and motivation, they can also join the Green Revolution.

The McDonalds junk is as good a place to start as any. The primary and highest priority is to get the HFCP out of the "food". Fortunately, when Coke comes up with an actual natural organic soda pop, it will automatically roll out to all of the McDonalds fast junk saloons, and they can start advertising that they are offering healthier food immediately. They will have to change the recipes for most of their fast junk products, such as the salad dressings, milkshakes and ketchup. Sadly, the ketchup is nearly a lost cause, so I am going to talk about Heinz after McDonalds.

Instead of buns made of highly refined white flour, they could go to whole wheat buns. I know what you are thinking. They will make horrible fast junk buns, and add just enough coloring and texturing to make them look like healthy bread, where actually the buns will still be fast junk. Rainbow and Wonder both have "whole wheat" versions of their bread, but they are fakes. The Classic Grilled Chicken Sandwich has a bun that looks like nice healthy whole wheat. I feed it to my dog.

Unfortunately, with McDonalds, the HFCP is only half of the issue. The meat they sell is produced in the most horrible way possible. The whole concept of producing and freezing food in one location and then shipping it to millions of fast junk saloons worldwide is a very bad idea. McDonalds will have to solve both of these problems, and neither one is small.

The individual McDonalds fast junk saloons will have to obtain local sources of free-ranged locally slaughtered ground beef. The way meat is processed by companies like Tyson's is simply unacceptable. McDonalds will have to buy their produce from locally run organic greenhouses, or build greenhouses themselves to produce the veggies they serve in their products. They can start offering napkins and paper products that are made from recycled material. Their fleet of delivery trucks would also have to be upgraded similarly to those of Coca Cola. Eventually, they could possibly produce their own electricity to reduce their dependency upon crude oil. It does seem to be a serious challenge, but even McDonalds can grow green! If they do that, we can go back to calling them fast food restaurants, instead of fast junk saloons, which is what they are now.

Of course, the healthy, organic green version of McDonalds that I have described is far different from the average McDonalds fast junk saloon of 2010. If one were to walk into this hypothetical McDonalds of the future, it would not look like the McDonald's of today. In fact, it wouldn't smell the same either. The odor of the food would be entirely different, because the ingredients would all be organic and locally produced. Their fast junk saloon chain would lose some consistency, but for the sake of selling healthy food instead of fast junk, it would be worth it. Profits will also go down, at least in the short run, but the corporations that want to survive will have to make sacrifices.

Ketchup appears to have been invented as a vehicle to deliver large amounts of sugar and HFCP into the human organism as quickly as possible. However, it occurs to me that ketchup must have been an actual food once upon a time, so I did a search on the internet and found the following recipe:

- 6 large tomatoes, quartered

- 1 bulb fennel, chopped

- 1 yellow onion, chopped

- 4 cloves garlic

- 1/4 cup raw organic sugar

- 1/4 cup molasses

- 1/4 cup red wine vinegar

- 10 whole cloves

- 2 whole star anise pods

- 1 tablespoon salt

Heinz would have to simply change to using a recipe like this one that does not contain HFCP. I know that they will also want to put in a preservative, but perhaps they could research finding an organic preservative.

A much more expensive endeavor would be the greening process of a major energy corporation, so I will use Exxon/Mobile for an example. This corporation has been built on the extraction, transportation, refinement and sale of crude oil. I am sure that like any corporation, they are going to want to survive over the next 20 years, even though they are in the worst possible position to go green of any corporation. Oil corporations are built upon the exploitation of a non-renewable resource, so the trick will be to migrate to a renewable energy source.

Wind energy is awesome for small-scale use, and hydro-electric technology is also a very excellent usage of the Earth's resources to produce energy. Unfortunately, neither of these sources will be able to supply the energy needs of the world today.

Solar energy is not only renewable, but exploits the most massive source of power in the solar system, one which is likely to be around for another few billion years. Once the investment has been made to create a large solar panel farm, it would pay off over and over again. With a little maintenance, such a solar farm would continue to supply electricity to America for hundreds of years to come. There are large sunny tracts of land in Texas that would be perfectly suitable for large solar energy farms.

Naturally, making this vision of Exxon/Mobile become reality would entail an enormous expense. As assets become obsolete and oil becomes scarcer, the company could capitalize on the sales of useless assets and invest that money in the new solar energy farms. Exxon/Mobile does have sufficient wealth to take on the research and development of more efficient solar cells. In the end, this corporation would depend only upon a constantly renewing energy supply, and provide said energy to the rest of America.

There are many kinds of corporations and companies in America, and I have discussed only a few. Using recycled paper products is one thing that all offices can do. If your company ships a product, you can start using recycled packing materials. If you do have a product that you ship, it should be obtained locally, to cut down on the use of crude oil. Every corporation will need to be analyzed on a case-by-case basis to develop a strategy for their individual greening process.

Chapter 7:
Green VS Red Corporations

The Green Scale is a means of measuring the degree of environmental friendliness of a corporation. The scale is from 0 to 10, and Exxon/Mobile is an example of a 0, as is Monsanto.

To get the perfect 10 rating, a company must create any resource that it consumes, not pollute, not abuse Humanity or the environment, produce only products and services that have a beneficial effect, and hold to morally high standards, such as not committing treason.

The Green Scale evaluation of a corporation includes an analysis of its inputs and outputs, in other words, the resources it consumes and the product(s)/service(s) that it produces, as well as any waste or byproducts of production.

Violations of the Green Standard are recorded as red flags on the corporation's evaluation report. The more red flags the corporation gets, the lower its rating on the Green Scale. Red flagged corporations symbolize a wound on the face of Mother Earth. They cause our planet to bleed resources as they abuse the environment and Humanity. Corporations will also get red flags for bribing congressmen. Putting HFCP in food and lying about it being poison also earns a corporation a red flag. Coke, Pepsi, McDonalds, Wal-Mart, Tyson's and Monsanto are all Red Corporations. Monsanto also messes with genetic engineering, another major red flag.

In order to pass the initial Green Scale inspection, a corporation's morals will be examined. Most of the evil MMC's have their priorities desperately out of order, as discussed in Chapter 2. The corporation's priorities will be compared with the list of morally correct priorities that follows:

1) Humanity
2) The Environment
3) Obeying the Law
4) Profit

Any corporation found guilty of putting profit ahead of Humanity gets the ultimate red flag. Greed will have to be put aside, or this deadly sin will kill us all. Corporations will be forced to choose between Greed and Green.

The greening process of a corporation is likely to take decades and not years, but each corporation will have a unique timeline to completion.

Upon completion of the corporation's initial evaluation process, they will be assigned a Green Scale star rating that represents where they presently stand. The company will then be analyzed in subsections divided up by department, and a strategy for prioritizing and implementing the greening process for each department will be developed, as well as timelines for effecting the changes.

The goal of every company will be to attain a ten star Green Scale rating, although many corporations will never get there. Even getting an evaluation demonstrates a positive attitude on the part of a corporation.

Chapter 8:
A Sustainable Human Existence

We are at a crucial juncture in human existence, but also are blessed to be alive at this time of change.

The transformation of Humanity is not so pronounced on the level of the physiology, as it is on the level of consciousness. This shift in consciousness leads to a change in the way Humanity perceives itself, its environment, and its place in the world and history.

As we look around us at the world in 2010, we see a world that is new and different, and the way we see it is also different. America has never been a very spiritual nation, like India, in spite of the fact that many of our citizens are religious. Religions are actually very negative spiritually, and tend to destroy one's covenant with Mother Nature and God.

To envision Humanity's place in the world, one must first focus one's attention on Mother Nature herself.

America, being a greed-based superficial society, tends to view the world on the physical surface level; this obscures the more refined levels of creation from sight. Rather than seeing a forest as an accumulation of trees and various flora and fauna, it should be seen as a network of spiritual energy fields filled with flying, dancing spirits. I call these spirits *sprites*, but they are actually various forms of fauna. To me, a bird or a minnow is a wild forest sprite. I own some forest land, and delight in my relationship to each and every form of life on my land.

When I first moved onto my farm, it had been used as a landfill, and was badly damaged from years of abuse. I have protected and nurtured the land, and the forest has grown. As Nature is nurtured, it becomes increasingly powerful. This strength of natural spiritual energy is what heals me, as I have also survived years of terrible abuse. Nature and I work together to protect and heal each other, and my place in the world becomes more apparent to me.

The place of Humanity in the world can be viewed similarly, but on a larger scale.

Rather than seeing the Earth as a complex network of biological systems, it should be seen as a living body. Since the industrial revolution, Humanity has taken the role of a parasite leaching off of the Earth, and doing more harm than good. It is time for

Humanity to take the role of a symbiote, living attached to the body of Mother Earth, but in a mutually beneficial relationship. Every corporation should become one of these organisms in a beneficial symbiotic relationship with the environment of the Earth.

Families and individuals can also see themselves in such a symbiotic relationship with Mother Earth. Each family can give themselves a Green Scale evaluation and try to reuse as much of their waste products as possible. For instance, I don't throw away newspapers or wrapping paper; I save them to use as kindling to get fires started in my wood-burning cook-stove. Aluminum containers can be ground into powder for use in pyrotechnics. Most waste produced by a family or individual can be reused in some way. Much of it is also recyclable.

Part of this symbiotic relationship with the Earth is also on the level of the human heart. If you love Mother Nature, then she will love you back. Apply the energies that you are capable of producing in a way that is nurturing to the environment as opposed to being destructive. See yourself as a mass of energy, not just a body with a spirit living inside of it.

With the change in perspective that accompanies the evolution of consciousness, individuals, families and corporations can all become beneficial members of the Earth's biosphere.

The bottom line is that the Earth is the only planet that we have to inhabit at this time. We are now realizing that it is not possible to destroy the Earth and still survive as a species. Our own survival is mutually dependent upon the survival of the Earth.

Any form of human society that destroys the Earth or is dependent upon non-renewable resources is ultimately doomed to extinction. In order to survive, we must find a way to meet our own biological needs without harming the Earth.

In order that our species can survive on the Earth in the long-term, we must learn to use our resources in an enlightened way. By using only what we create, and by working with the power of Mother Nature, we can heal our own wounds and those of our planet simultaneously. A sustainable human existence is the *only* possible human existence in the long run.

Chapter 9:
Summary and Conclusion

The corporation originated as an innocent means for people to work together towards a common goal and be seen as a single entity in the eyes of the law.

Due to the inherent greed of a Capitalistic human society, corporations have manipulated our government into granting them absurd amounts of power. The Multinational Mega-Corporations are now the most powerful, dangerous and corrupt entities in the history of the planet Earth. They also pose a direct threat to the future of Humanity. They are life-sucking vampires with their teeth sunk deeply into the planet on which we live, and are going to continue to drink Mother Nature's blood until they have sucked her to death.

The cause of the corruption of the corporations over time is due to the way that they have been defined legally. Their only priority is profit, motivated by the evil of greed. The MMC's have sacrificed any claim to morality by threatening the Earth and Humanity.

To rectify the morality of the corporations, they should be required to make Humanity their highest priority, the environment next, and then obeying the law, all before making a profit. Instead of fining criminal corporations, which is useless, their corporate charters should be revoked. The most important corporate charter to revoke is that of Monsanto; they are Satan itself. Boycotting the stocks and products of red corporations who commit crimes against Humanity is also an effective means of striking at these monsters. Destroying public confidence in the MMC's brand names also causes them to lose value. If all else fails, they can also be attacked militarily.

On the other hand, as the collective consciousness of America evolves, so do the corporations out of necessity. Although some pretend to be growing green and are actually lying about it, some are actually making a sincere effort. Corporations can get a Green Scale evaluation and analysis to help them establish a process for modifying their systems to become environmentally friendly. If the MMC's are going to survive the Green Revolution and the change in Humanity's collective consciousness, they are going to have to make themselves part of a sustainable human existence. Pepsi and McDonalds alike are going to have to start offering fully organic products, use recycled products, and become self-sufficient in terms of the resources they consume.

As human consciousness continues to evolve, the way we see the world and our place in it also changes. The world is not just a resource to be exploited, but it is also a spiritual being with whom we are in a symbiotic relationship. It is important that people and corporations alike form a beneficial relationship with Mother Earth, rather than consuming it for selfish purposes.

By living symbiotically with the Earth rather than parasitically, we can build a sustainable existence for our species.